ANIMALS
That Make a Difference!

Squirrels
다람쥐

Ashley Lee

Explore other books at:
WWW.ENGAGEBOOKS.COM

VANCOUVER, B.C.

e WWW.ENGAGEBOOKS.COM

Squirrels: Level 1 Bilingual (English/Korean) (영어/한국어)
Animals That Make a Difference!
Lee, Ashley 1995 –
Text © 2021 Engage Books
Edited by: A.R. Roumanis and Lauren Dick
Translated by: Gio Oh
Proofread by: Tamara Kazali

Text set in Arial Regular.
Chapter headings set in Arial Black.

FIRST EDITION / FIRST PRINTING

LIBRARY AND ARCHIVES CANADA CATALOGUING IN PUBLICATION

Title: Animals That Make a Difference: Squirrels Level 1 Bilingual (English/Korean) (영어/한국어)
Names: Lee, Ashley, author.

ISBN 978-1-77476-465-7 (hardcover)
ISBN 978-1-77476-464-0 (softcover)

Subjects:
LCSH: Squirrels—Juvenile literature
LCSH: Human-animal relationships—Juvenile literature

Classification: LCC QL737.R68 L44 2020 | DDC J599.36—DC23

Contents
목차

What Are Squirrels?
다람쥐는 무엇인가요?

Squirrels are rodents.
다람쥐는 설치류 입니다.

Rodents have long front teeth.
설치류는 긴 앞니를 가지고 있습니다.

What Do Squirrels Look Like?
다람쥐는 어떻게 생겼나요?

The largest squirrels are 3 feet (1 meter) long from their nose to the end of their tail. The smallest squirrels are only 5 inches (13 centimeters) long.

가장 큰 다람쥐는 코부터 꼬리까지 3피트(1미터) 입니다. 가장 작은 다람쥐는 5인치(13센티미터) 입니다.

A squirrel's tail is long and bushy.
다람쥐의 꼬리는 길고 숱이 많아요.

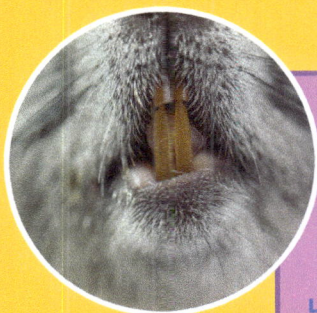

Squirrels have sharp front teeth that never stop growing.
다람쥐는 계속 자라나는 날카로운 앞니가 있어요.

Squirrels have four fingers on each front paw. They also have short thumbs for gripping.
다람쥐는 한 발에 손가락이 네개 있어요. 물건을 잡는 용도로 짧은 엄지도 있어요.

Where Do Squirrels Live?
다람쥐는 어디에서 사나요?

Squirrels live all over the world. The only place they are not found is in Australia. Some squirrels live in trees and some live underground.
다람쥐는 전 세계에 다 삽니다. 하지만 호주에서는 다람쥐를 찾아볼 수 없습니다. 몇몇 다람쥐는 나무에서 살지만 몇몇은 지하에 삽니다.

Three-striped palm squirrels are found in India and Sri Lanka. Japanese dwarf flying squirrels can only be found in Japan.
세줄야자다람쥐는 인도나 스리랑카에 삽니다. 일본 난쟁이 날다람쥐는 일본에서만 찾아 볼 수 있습니다.

Atlantic Ocean
북극해

Japan
일본

Europe
유럽

Asia
아시아

India
인도

Pacific Ocean
태평양

Africa
아프리카

Indian Ocean
인도양

Atlantic Ocean
대서양

Sri Lanka
스리랑카

Southern Ocean
남대양

2,000 miles
2,000 마일
0

0
4,000 kilometers
4,000 킬로미터

N

Legend 전설
Land 육지
Ocean 바다

9

What Do Squirrels Eat?
다람쥐는 무엇을 먹나요?

Squirrels mostly eat nuts, seeds, and plants. They also eat small insects, fruit, and tree sap.
다람쥐는 대부분 견과류, 씨앗 그리고 식물을 먹어요. 또한 작은 곤충, 과일 그리고 나무 수액을 먹기도해요.

Some squirrels hide their food.
They bury it in the soil for later.
몇몇 다람지들은 음식을 숨겨요.
나중을 위해서 흙 밑에 숨겨요.

How Do Squirrels Talk to Each Other?
다람쥐는 서로 어떻게 이야기하나요?

Squirrels make sounds to call other squirrels or warn them of danger. Some squirrels will scream when they are scared.

다람쥐는 다른 다람쥐를 부르거나 위험을 경고하기 위해서 소리를 내요. 몇몇 다람쥐는 겁에 질리면 소리를 지른답니다.

Squirrels wave their tails back and forth when they are attacked. This makes them look bigger and can scare other animals.

다람쥐는 공격을 받았을 때 꼬리를 앞뒤로 흔들어요. 이 행동은 몸집을 더 커보이게하고 다른 동물을 위협할 수 있답니다.

Squirrel Life Cycle
다람쥐의 일생

Baby squirrels are born hairless and blind. Their eyes stay closed for about one month.
아기 다람쥐는 털과 시력이 없는채로 태어나요. 한달 동안 눈을 감은채 지내요.

Young squirrels cannot leave their mother's nest for about 40 days.
아기 다람쥐는 40일 동안 엄마의 둥지를 떠나지 못해요.

Young squirrels make their own nests when they are about two months old.
아기 다람쥐는 2달정도가 지나면 자기만의 둥지를 만들어요.

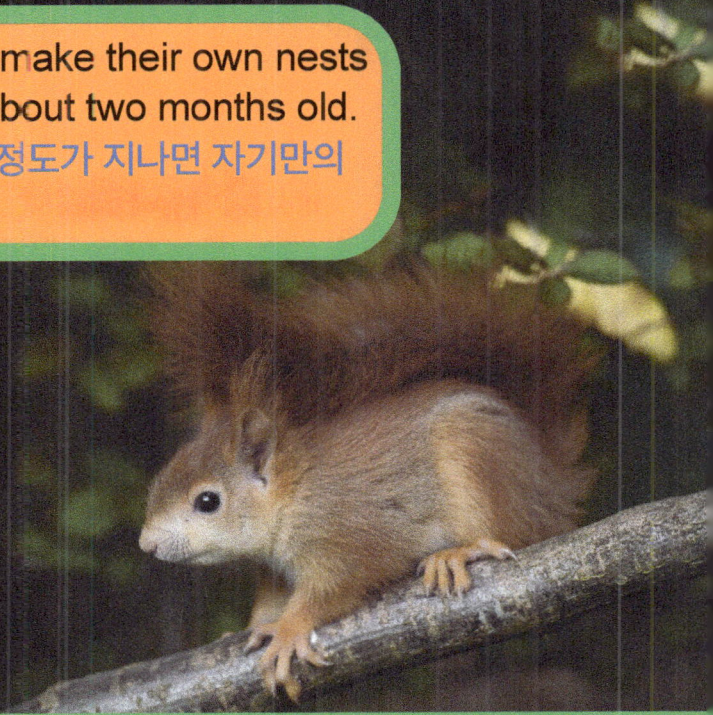

Some types of squirrels live longer than others. Eastern gray squirrels can live for up to 12 years. Tiny antelope ground squirrels only live for about one year.
어떤 종류의 다람쥐는 다른 종보다 오래살아요. 회색 큰 다람쥐는 최대 12년까지 살 수 있어요. 작은 영양 땅 다람쥐는 약 1년정도만 살 수 있어요.

15

Curious Facts About Squirrels

Some squirrels sort their food into groups before burying it. They may sort their nuts by type or size.
어떤 다람쥐들은 먹이를 묻기전 분류를 해요.
견과류의 종류나 크기가 기준이 될 거에요.

Squirrels sometimes pretend to bury their nuts. This is meant to trick any thieves who may be watching.
가끔 다람쥐는 먹이를 묻는 척을 합니다. 지켜보고 있을 수도 있는 도둑을 속이기 위해서이죠.

Squirrels can find their buried food under one foot of snow.
다람쥐는 한 발 눈 아래에 묻혀있는 먹이도 찾을 수 있습니다.

다람쥐에 대한 흥미로운 사실들

Some squirrels have pouches in their cheeks for storing food.
어떤 다람쥐들은 먹이를 저장하기 위해 볼안에 먹이주머니가 있습니다.

Squirrels are one of the few animals that can run down a tree head first.
다람쥐는 나무 머리를 타고 내려올 수 있는 몇 안되는 동물입니다.

Squirrels were a common pet in North America about 200 years ago.
200년전 북아메리카에서 다람쥐는 흔한 애완동물이었습니다.

Kinds of Squirrels
다람쥐의 종류

There are more than 250 different kinds of squirrels.These are split into three groups. The squirrels in each group are similar.

다람쥐는 250종이 넘습니다. 이는 세가지로 분류 할 수 있습니다. 같이 분류된 다람쥐들은 비슷합니다.

Tree squirrels are the most common type of squirrel. They live in trees and are great climbers.

나무 다람쥐는 다람쥐 중에서 가장 흔한 종입니다. 나무안에 살고 훌륭한 등산가입니다.

Flying squirrels have a thin layer of skin between their front and back legs. This acts like a pair of wings when they jump between trees.
날다람쥐는 앞다리와 뒷다리에 아주 얇은 가죽이 있습니다. 이는 나무 사이로 뛰어다닐 때 날개와 비슷한 역할을 합니다.

Ground squirrels live underground. They are often found in large groups.
땅다람쥐는 지하에서 삽니다. 여러마리로 뭉쳐다니는 것이 자주 발견됩니다.

How Squirrels Help Other Animals
다람쥐가 다른 동물을 돕는 방법

Squirrels are food for other animals.
다람쥐는 다른 동물의 먹이가 될 수 있습니다.

There would be less wolves, snakes, and large birds without squirrels for them to eat.
다람쥐가 없다면 늑대, 뱀, 그리고 큰 새들이 먹을 먹이가 줄어들 것입니다.

How Squirrels Help Earth
다람쥐가 지구를 돕는 방법

Squirrels bury nuts and seeds in many different spots. Sometimes squirrels cannot remember where they hid their food.

다람쥐는 다양한 곳에 견과류나 씨앗을 묻어놓습니다. 가끔 다람쥐는 먹이 숨겨놓은 곳을 찾지 못할 때도 있습니다.

Some buried nuts and seeds grow into new plants. Many plants would not grow without help from forgetful squirrels.

몇몇 견과류나 씨앗은 새로운 식물로 자라기도 합니다. 다람쥐가 이를 잊지않았다면 많은 식물들은 자라나지 못했을 것입니다.

How Squirrels Help Humans
다람쥐가 사람을 돕는 방법

Some squirrels hibernate during the winter. This means they sleep until the weather gets warmer.

어떤 다람쥐들은 겨울 동안 겨울잠을 잡니다. 이는 날이 따뜻해질 때까지 잠을 잔다는 것을 의미합니다.

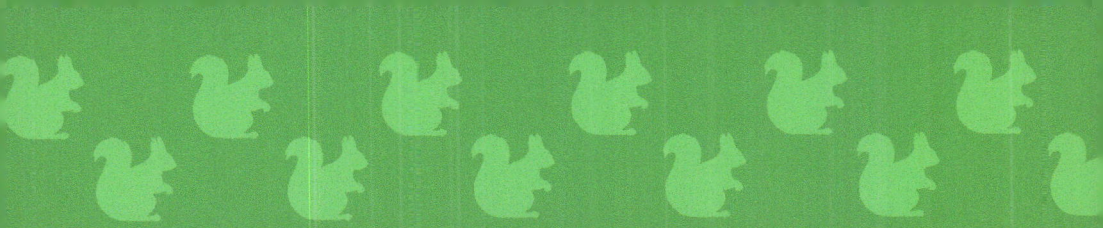

Scientists are studying how squirrels hibernate. This may help them make new medicine for people with heart problems.

과학자들은 다람쥐가 어떻게 겨울잠을 자는지 연구해요. 이는 심장 질환이 있는 사람들을 도울 새로운 약을 만드는데 도움이 될 수도 있습니다.

Squirrels in Danger
멸종위기의 다람쥐

Red squirrels are endangered. This means there are very few of them left.
붉은 다람쥐는 멸종위기에 처했어요. 이는 붉은 다람쥐가 많이 남지 않았다는 것을 뜻합니다.

Red squirrels live in England, Wales, Ireland, and Scotland. Gray squirrels were brought to these countries from North America. They brought a germ with them that harms red squirrels.

붉은 다람쥐는 영국, 웨일즈, 아일랜드 그리고 스코틀랜드에서 왔어요. 회색다람쥐는 북미에서 왔지요. 회색다람쥐는 붉은 다람쥐를 해칠 수 있는 세균을 가지고 왔어요.

How To Help Squirrels
다람쥐를 돕는 방법

Garbage can end up in places animals live. Squirrels can get hurt if they get trapped in a piece of garbage. They can also get sick if they try to eat it.

쓰레기가 동물이 사는 곳 까지 다다를 수 있어요. 쓰레기에 갇혀서 다람쥐들이 다칠 수도 있어요. 쓰레기를 먹어서 병이 날 수 도 있어요.

Many people are cleaning forests. They pick up garbage and take it to a landfill. This helps keep squirrels safe.

많은 사람들이 숲을 치우고 있어요. 쓰레기를 주워서 매립지에 가지고 갑니다. 이는 다람쥐들을 지키는데 도움이 돼요.

Quiz
퀴즈

Test your knowledge of squirrels by answering the following questions. The questions are based on what you have read in this book. The answers are listed on the bottom of the next page.

다음 질문에 답하고 상어에 대한 지식을 테스트해봐요. 질문은 책의 내용에 기초합니다. 정답은 다음 페이지 하단에 있어요.

1 What is the only place squirrels are not found?
다람쥐를 찾을 수 없는 유일한 장소는 어디인가요?

2 What do some squirrels do when they are scared?
다람쥐는 무서울 때 어떻게 하나요?

3 How long do a baby squirrel's eyes stay closed?
아기 다람쥐는 눈을 감은채 얼마나 있나요?

4 How do squirrels sometimes trick thieves?
다람쥐가 도둑을 어떻게 속이나요?

5 How many different kinds of squirrels are there?
다람쥐는 몇 종류가 있나요?

6 What does it mean when squirrels hibernate during winter?
다람쥐가 겨울 잠을 잔다는 것은 무슨 뜻인가요?

Explore other books in the Animals That Make a Difference series.

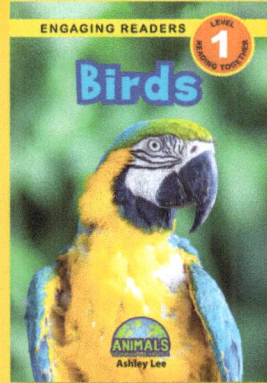

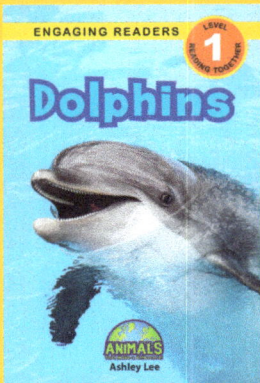

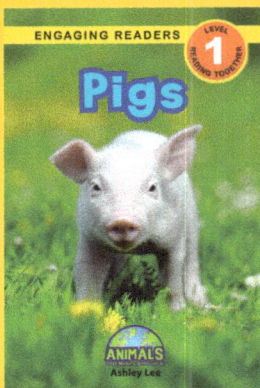

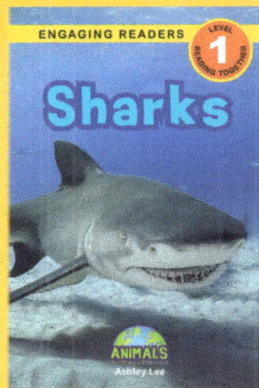

ENGAGING READERS — LEVEL 1 — READING TOGETHER
Bees
ANIMALS
Jared Siemens

ENGAGING READERS — LEVEL 1 — READING TOGETHER
Bats
ANIMALS
Ashley Lee

ENGAGING READERS — LEVEL 1 — READING TOGETHER
Birds
ANIMALS
Ashley Lee

ENGAGING READERS — LEVEL 1 — READING TOGETHER
Dolphins
ANIMALS
Ashley Lee

ENGAGING READERS — LEVEL 1 — READING TOGETHER
Horses
ANIMALS
Ashley Lee

ENGAGING READERS — LEVEL 1 — READING TOGETHER
Lady Bugs
ANIMALS
Ashley Lee

ENGAGING READERS — LEVEL 1 — READING TOGETHER
Pigs
ANIMALS
Ashley Lee

ENGAGING READERS — LEVEL 1 — READING TOGETHER
Sharks
ANIMALS
Ashley Lee

ENGAGING READERS — LEVEL 1 — READING TOGETHER
Squirrels
ANIMALS
Ashley Lee

Visit www.engagebooks.com to explore more Engaging Readers.

정답: 1. 호주 2. 비명 지르기 3. 약 한달 4. 자신들 몫의 견과류 숨기기 5. 250종 이상 6. 뭐이 따뜻해질 때까지 잠자기

Answers: 1. Australia 2. Scream 3. About one month 4. They pretend to bury their nuts 5. More than 250 6. They sleep until the weather gets warmer

www.ingramcontent.com/pod-product-compliance
Lightning Source LLC
Chambersburg PA
CBHW051240020426
42331CB00016B/3463